YOUR KNOWLEDGE HAS VALUE

Bibliographic information published by the German National Library:

The German National Library lists this publication in the National Bibliography; detailed bibliographic data are available on the Internet at http://dnb.dnb.de .

Imprint:

Copyright © 1998 GRIN Verlag
Print and binding: Books on Demand GmbH, Norderstedt Germany
ISBN: 9783668969834

Miki Garcia

Wish you weren't here. Tourism and child prostitution in Thailand

GRIN Verlag

GRIN - Your knowledge has value

Since its foundation in 1998, GRIN has specialized in publishing academic texts by students, college teachers and other academics as e-book and printed book. The website www.grin.com is an ideal platform for presenting term papers, final papers, scientific essays, dissertations and specialist books.

Visit us on the internet:

http://www.grin.com/

http://www.facebook.com/grincom

http://www.twitter.com/grin_com

Wish You Weren't Here:

Tourism and Child Prostitution in Thailand

Submitted to the Department of Journalism in part-fulfilment of the requirements for the degree of Master of Arts in International Journalism

City University

September 1998

TABLE OF CONTENTS

PROJECT

Young girls in supply, and the demand seems limitless

The commercial sexual exploitation of girls is a global, multi-billion dollar industry, pouring money into the hands of private citizens, tourists, governments and the police. No single approach, in a single country, can entirely solve the problem. Miki Garcia on how to cope with this international hazards.

'We are born crying, not laughing.' A Thai proverb says: Life is a struggle from start to finish. For many girls in Bangkok, these words reflect reality. In some Thai villages, girls are dragged out of school and sold for the price of a television set, and forced to work in brothels. They become the bikinied schoolgirls swinging and dancing provocatively on the catwalks of the city's numerous bars and the playthings of foreigners and Thais. The commercial sexual exploitation of girls or child prostitutes is not a new phenomenon but it is now a global, organised and growing industry.

'The recent phenomenon is that overall number of prostitutes is decreasing but child prostitution is increasing. As a direct result of the Asian economic crisis, children are cheaper to hire. The economic crisis has changed the whole situation in Thailand, economically, politically and socially,' Chris Beddoe, campaign co-ordinator of London-based charity End Child Prostitution in Asian Tourism (ECPAT) UK, said in an interview. Due to the nature of work, there are no reliable statistics. Children are the hidden side of an illegal industry. But UNICEF estimates that there are at least one million children in prostitution in Asia alone. Law enforcement by Thai authorities and extraterritorial legislation in the UK are proving ineffective in eliminating this problem. The child sex industry developed partly as a response to demand from tourists. Partly, it is a result of a proactive attempt to induce demand by creating supply. Child sex tourism means lucrative business for many people including hotel owners and taxi drivers, but never for the children. 'Tourism cannot only provide the opportunity for the systematic abuser (paedophile) but can also provide the situational abuser (opportunistic) with the circumstances which promote their abuse. It is vital that the public are aware that such behaviour is not acceptable in developing countries,' said Ms Beddoe. Poor countries are under economic pressure to develop tourism as a source of income. World-wide travel has increased sevenfold since 1960, according to ECPAT data, which suggests tourism will soon be the biggest industry globally. Child sex tourism is now part of this world-wide business.

For most people a holiday means 'having a break'. But for some Britons and others, it means 'engaging in sexual activities with children'. There are an estimated 110,000 convicted male paedophiles in England and Wales, according to a Home Office study. 'It is as though these men, a lot of whom come from the West, believe they are entitled to come and buy whatever they want in a poor country and that the children should be grateful because they get some money,' said Dr. Kitija Phornsadja, Project Director for UNICEF in Bangkok. According to the ECPAT international headquarters in Bangkok, there were about 20,000 child prostitutes in 1991. By 1996, there were 250,000. The evidence supports the belief that as the tourism industry expands there is a parallel expansion of child sex tourism. The report states that individuals who see the sexual exploitation of children as some sort of hobby or sport, supply information on new locations, prices and even individual children for free, to others like themselves, increasingly by using hard to control internet technology. You can get any kind of information through the internet. For instance, a novice who doesn't not know how to find a girl can open the site (http://fantasyisles.com/). It recommends a book called *Fantasy Islands: A Man's Guide to Exotic Women and International Travel*, or *The Gentlemen's Guide*, which will tell you how to make friends with 'useful information'. After arriving in Bangkok, the easiest way to meet the right people is to go to a bar. Instantly, locals will approach you with loads of trivia. Small-scale travel operators, very often one man outfits, can instantly arrange sex travels and indicate the resorts where prostitution is easily available. They can make arrangements - a 24-hour companion or show you the hotels known to tolerate or actively promote prostitution. Customers can choose child escorts from catalogue pictures. On top of that, they can easily provide a vehicle for travelling sex tourists. Travel arrangements for the vast majority of sex tourists are organised by reputable local travel agents and package tour operators. Sex tourists are transported by ordinary airlines. The marketing material by many reputable travel companies helps sustain the flow, often stressing the attractions of night life, promulgating stereotypes about Third-World-people as 'smiling', 'laid back', and 'exotic'. A Dutch travel agency offers some pictures of children on the travel brochures, smiling and wearing traditional Thai dresses. A girl wearing a make up sits in a temple, and the leaflet reads: 'You can get the feeling that taking a girl here is as easy as buying a package of cigarettes. Little slaves who give real Thai warmth.' According to the Real Man's Mid-life Crisis Tour of Thailand, which actually exists, and operates out of San Diego, US: 'I recently had a 79-year old customer who visited Thailand after a by-pass operation and he had sex three times a day with prostitutes aged between 15- and 19-year-old. I tell you it almost brought tears in my eyes.' Unfortunately, this kind of 'Real Man's' tour exists all over the world. Newspapers in almost major cities of the world have open advertisements for tours to Asia whose purpose is to provide travellers sex with local girls. In Bangkok hotels, the Yellow Pages offer loads of advertisements. Organised sex tours that have been identified by ECPAT exist in Australia, France, Japan, Germany, the

Netherlands, Norway, Sweden, Switzerland, the UK and the US. ECPAT also claims that paedophile travellers to Asia now have very well-established links. Many have a permanent residency in Thailand or other Asian cities, either as a retiree or a small business owner. From their base, they have devised ways to assist their friends from their home countries. In some cases, paedophile clubs in Europe have bought guest houses on the beach front for their members, and other long-staying paedophiles have opened homes for street children.

But why do people want to have sex with children? The anonymity the tourist enjoys abroad might release them from the social constraints of their home countries. According to the ECPAT report, in 'exotic' destinations, tourists usually don't understand the language or the nuances in the society which can lead to assumptions, that sex with children is accepted there, or as another rationalisation, that commercial sex is a way to help children getting out of poverty. It also suggests that tourists from industrialised states, holding menial positions at home, are often 'rich' in their destination country. And this comparative wealth often changes their behaviour patterns.

'I know a Swedish guy who works in a Sweden Embassy in Bangkok. If you want to get information on prostitutes, give him a ring,' said 'former-Londoner' Jeremy Ruggrok, 61. According to him, he has many contacts, because 'he is working for the Sweden Embassy'. Jeremy claimed that a man called Leif Alstead who works in the embassy got lots of information, but after contacting the Sweden Embassy in London later, it denied his existence saying that he was not on the Foreign Ministry's list. Jeremy complained that he has recently lost his wallet. He said he didn't even remember why or where he lost it, perhaps his one-night young employee took it. Wearing a singlet and baggy shirts, he proudly shows off his tattoos in Thai on his arms. 'I didn't like England. I used to have a flat in South Kensington. I worked at an estate agency in London, then I went to Zimbabwe and stayed there for several years and worked as a baker. I didn't like that country very much.' And he came to Mae Sai, Thailand about 10 years ago. 'I love this country. Nice climate, nice people. I am usually based in Phuket. There are 5,000 strong British community there,' he said proudly. Asked whether he finally felt like settling there, he said: 'Yeah, I think so. But I might go to Cambodia.' According to ECPAT, Cambodia has actually been marketed by illegal travel agencies as a paedophile haven, and the number of child prostitutes has been increasing sharply. He sits in the bar from 11 o'clock in the morning doing absolutely nothing but chatting with his mates from the US, the Netherlands, France, Sweden who are in the same situation. Asked why he likes Thai girls, he said, 'All of my previous girlfriends have been Asians. I like their dark long hair and skin complexion. Age really doesn't matter.' There is a popular saying amongst paedophiles: 'Age is not the problem. The point is one is able to have sex or not.'

The root cause is not straightforward. There are so many business interests coming from all directions. But to combat child sex tourism, the co-operation of the tourism industry is essential. Last year, the Association of British Travel Agents (ABTA), ECPAT, Britain's Home Office, Foreign and Commonwealth Office and HM Customs & Excise jointly produced an information leaflet on the introduction of extra territorial jurisdiction for British citizens. Tourism industry workers including tour guides, taxi drivers and room maids are in strong positions to gather information which would assist in the prosecution of those who commit crimes against children. Debbie Gibson, press officer of ABTA claims, 'our campaign with ECPAT and others is doing well to bring awareness within the UK. If you don't show the commitment with tourism, hotels, transport, and so on, you will never get rid of child sex tourism.' ABTA has been promoting the message 'there is no escape from prosecution' through its members. Legislation, granting courts the power to try people for abusing children overseas has been introduced. For example, Co-op Travelcare which is an ABTA member, printed and distributed its own leaflets advising that 'sex with a child is a crime.' 'Education from the tourist industry could prevent such behaviour,' said Ms Gibson.

The Northern region is the poorest area of the country. The area was once known as the 'golden triangle' but is now dubbed the 'golden quadrangle.' New roads across the green hillsides are signs of a boom economy. The Mekong development project along the Mekong river is under way amongst four countries – Thailand, China, Laos and Burma. This notorious drug smuggling area is now aiming at economic growth. The Mekong is not only a river of hope for millions people, but it is also a focal point for the trafficking in women and children, which has increased rapidly in the past few years. According to ECPAT, trafficking of children is bigger than the drug trade. The number of children brought to work as prostitutes in Thailand from neighbouring Burma and Cambodia is over 10,000 each year, according to another report by the Centre for the Protection of Children's Rights (CPCR), a Bangkok-based non-governmental organisation (NGO). 'In the Mekong Development Project, along with the building up roads and dams, urbanisation and environmental degradation means structural changes for families and rural communities. It may become more vulnerable to the effects of poverty and exploitation especially for the poor and the hill tribe people,' said Wanlop Pichpongsa, operation officer of Population and Community Development Association (PDA) based in Mae Sai. 'The Mekong development project can cause many things, both good and bad. There will be a black market in goods, smuggling and drug trafficking. Also, prostitution trends to increase.'

The Thai government is as ever keen to encourage tourism. Seree Wangpaichitr, the governor of the Tourism Authority of Thailand said: 'Over the next few years, the Mekong region will see intensive road-building, tremendous development of airports and airlines, and mega-million dollar investments in other infrastructure. This will bring business, conventions and holiday travel.' But Mr Pichpongsa acknowledges that materialism has increased with the region's development. This encourages families to sell their daughters into prostitution to buy a new television set or to build a house. The business of child prostitution in Thailand is changing with these developments. Girls from neighbouring countries such as Burma and Cambodia come into Thailand, while girls who previously worked in a big city like Bangkok, go abroad to Japan, Europe, North America and Australia. Thailand is now both an exporting and a receiving country of girls for the sex trade.

According to ECPAT report, while the sexual exploitation of Thai girls seems to be declining, the cross-border trafficking of women and children from neighbouring countries has increased. The age of the children involved is also dropping. A UNICEF report reads children as young as five are being treated like commodities – taken from their homes and families to work in brothels, massage parlours, clubs and bars, or as private playthings for those who buy them like goods in a supermarket. 'If we accept a world in which children can be bought and sold as if they are goods in a supermarket, we forfeit the right to call ourselves civilised,' said Ron O'Grady, chair of ECPAT International. The fact of this flesh trade is that children who have no education, are forced to service anyone they are told. 'So this often involves children being forced to take part in sadistic acts, group sex and all kinds of perversion,' said Ms. Beddoe. Children are beaten and tortured if they refuse to comply. And they may never see their families again. Mr O'Grady pointed out that the organised child sex business is a recent phenomenon. Ms. Abueva agrees: 'The problem is that many local men have begun aping the tourists. It's part of the colonial mentality - if it is good for Western tourists, then it must be good for local men, too.' The UNICEF report also notes that it is a death sentence, for half of all child prostitutes are estimated to be HIV positive. 'Many men believe that sex with a child prostitute carries less risk of AIDS infection. This is a fallacy,' said Amihan Abueva, a former executive director of ECPAT. 'To most people in Asia, these men are unwanted parasites. They use the children as they wish and they fly out of the country, leaving behind the waste of broken young lives and the social catastrophe of AIDS and other sexually-transmitted diseases,' Mr O'Grady sums up the voice of innocent children.

Mae Sai, the northernmost point of Thailand is a lively town, full of energy, like any other border town. Trading people come and go across into Tachileck, a Burmese border town, carrying huge wicker baskets. In the market, the signs are written in Thai, Burmese and Chinese and people yelling in those languages at customers. But the town has a completely different face at night. 'It's better not to go out at night. Many local people have been murdered by drug dealers and traffickers. After they are killed, they are thrown into the

Mae Sai river,' said Julie Stratford, a Mae Sai-based Australian aid worker. This is the area where a substantial young prostitutes are coming from. At night, almost no one is on the streets except those going to clandestine meetings. Ghost town-like Mae Sai has some 70 entertainment spots – brothels, meeting pubs, karaoke bars and massage parlours. You can see Tachileck town's bright neon light from the Mae Sai side. Teenage girls stand along with pimps – chubby face with white thick power and vivid smudged lips. They are often in residential areas which creates an unusual atmosphere. Customers come from not only the local area but from abroad through highly organised tours. The pubs charge no entry fee and you can stay as long as you want. Just order a glass of beer (30 Baht about 50p – £1 = B60) until you find the girl you want. 'If you are young and beautiful, you can be paid around B1000 (about £167) a night. If not, the price goes down B300, B200...or less,' said Prakran Nilnet, 26, a local aid worker, who took me around and showed me the entertaining spots by motor bike. As we strolled around midnight, I came across Japanese and American tourists.

The origin of child sexual abuse is complex. Poverty is a major catalyst. And lack of education and job opportunities, criminal networks, amongst other things. Girls are more vulnerable than boys as they are seen as less valuable according to traditional perceptions. Minority ethnic groups are also vulnerable because they have different culture, language, value systems and various other issues. Parents sell daughters because there is no other means to earn money. Behind these attitudes, there is a lenient Buddhism philosophy based on gender bias such as daughter's expectations and responsibilities to the families which dominate the whole Thai way of life. According to Buddhist philosophy, sex is not a sin which is tied to the natural world, the world of suffering and ignorance. The Buddhist ideology is also linked to the concepts of 'merit making'. Such thought can rationalise that working as commercial sex workers means that they are helping their poor family financially, and the men believe that they are also helping poor girls. 'Most child sexual abuses are reported which suggest the criminals are fathers, step-fathers, relatives, and neighbours,' said Mr. Pichpongsa. Mikel Flamm, a Bangkok-based freelance journalist, also points out: 'In Thailand especially, children are taught to do as their parents tell them and if it means to be sold to a brothel or to go with a stranger the parents may not even know. It is often a choice they have no control over. They become caught in a web they often just accept.'

It was just after 1 am. There was a loud hubbub in the door next to my hotel room in the capital's inner suburb Sukumvit. 'Don't do this! Why are you doing this to me,' a girl screamed. 'I am dying.' A man with French accent shouted: 'I am your client. I am paying B2,000 for the night.' And the girl started crying uncontrollably. Then, something hit the wall. 'Why, why are you doing this to me.' For girls at work, every night is a matter of survival.

In the lurid neon lights of Patpond Road, the centre of Bangkok, there is a dense cluster of go-go bars, explicit nude bars, massage parlours, alongside stalls selling food and fake designer clothes. Girls on the street distinguish men's nationalities instantly. 'G'day mate,' to Australians, 'Guten tag,' to Germans, and 'Ilashaimase,' to the Japanese. With such an image, Patpong has world attention as 'The Asia's brothel.' When I went to Nana Plaza, the second biggest red-light district in Bangkok with Mr. Flamm for my project. It was during Songkran, Thailand's new year water festival in April. The area was packed with western men – some in their early-twenties or teens, others with big guts, some gorgeous-looking, others clearly retired – in the outdoor beer gardens. Men were screaming and running with baggy shirts holding water pistols, just like young boys. They were throwing water at girls and screaming in a shrill voice. Not barrier, no shame, no need for proper conversations because local girls there hardly speak English. It seems like they had become completely different personalities on a different planet. And they looked extremely happy. Bouncers solicited us to watch the 'sex show of the night'. Girls with chubby faces were using their bodies as attractively as possible in order to get customers. Age ranged between 10 and 20. About 20 girls were dancing on stage. They change every 10 minutes and different girls show up. Entering the bar is free, a glass of beer costs about 30 Baht. You can stay as long as you like, enjoy the show, find a girl. At 11pm, the tonight's show started. Some entertainer girls who perform on stage can get paid more than go-go girls. A girl on the shabby stage smiled at me sympathetically – probably she thought I was a prostitute as I was with an American man. She probably thought that we were on the same boat. I couldn't really smile back. Mark King, 30-year-old businessman from England has been based in South East Asia for four years, observes the situation: 'People who want to have sex might be fed up with strong western women. They might have had family and educational problems when they were growing up. They weren't loved by their own parents. They are looking for affection. They are also attracted by Asian girls' skin and dark hair. Plus their hospitality. Would you like some more? Are you tired? - they feel that at least somebody cares. But they treat Thai girls as a doormat.'

The Daughters' Education Programme (DEP) is a NGO which provides education opportunities for girls in Mae Sai. Providing sponsorship for girls in their early teens can keep them off the streets and enhance their ability to find alternative employment later. The DEP identifies girls who are at risk from being sold into the profitable prostitution trade. They also try to be one step ahead of the agents who come to the villages with money to tempt parents to sell their daughters. It gives opportunities to young girls to stay in school till the final year of primary school. DEP sponsors vocational training as well. 'Girls in the north have been exploited by society, by irresponsible adults and the people they trust,

9

including their own parents,' said Sompop Jantraka who started the programme. 'These girls have enormous potential to improve. All they need is opportunities to learn, and to live in a stable community. Education is the way to give them the confidence and the ability to decide their own future.' Mr Jantraka tells the parents what really happens to their children when they are sold. 'But we also have to help them - if their girls come to us they would have a means of earning when they finished, because families are desperately poor in these places and it is a tradition for daughters to go to work to support them.'

There are many community-based projects that fight against the commercial sexual exploitation of children. Prevention increases children's awareness of their rights. Recovery programmes help the children who have been abused. The important thing is to provide children alternative jobs so that they may stop working as prostitutes. 'Their work generates positive repercussion for the welfare of children,' said Rarinthip Sirorat, chief of the foreign relations sub-division, in the Thai Department of Public Welfare. But despite this effort, many girls who often have only little education go back to work as prostitutes. 'To those who are given the chance to learn a trade, this is a hard change for them and very often does not work, and they often last only a short time then go back to what they know best,' Mr. Flamm pints out. 'It is very difficult to explain to a girl who is used to making close to $100 per night to take a salary cut and make less than half of that. To the older girls who have been in the business for long periods of time, it becomes an addiction in away. There is an old saying: 'you can take the girl out of the bar, but you can't take the bar out of the girl. Many girls are addicted to drugs as well.'

Mr Pichpongsa also echoes this sentiment: 'I have to admit that many agencies – both governmental and NGOs – have failed the occupational training. One reason is that they didn't consider what is suitable for a particular community.' Atchara Chan-O-Kul of the Centre for the Protection of Children's Rights (CPCR), based in Bangkok, agrees: 'For example, there is a girl who trained as a hairdresser. But she can't make money as a hairdresser in her local village. Because there is no demand for it.' NGOs have to look at what is of benefit to local community and how to use their skills rather than let girls learn the new technology which is far away from their culture.' In some situations, a hairdresser runs the brothel in the back of the shop, or upstairs while giving customers a massage. Ms Beddoe also points out that the need is not always for traditional gendered jobs which can be biased against earning the same money as men but a much broader all-round training to allow women to progress socially and economically. Ms Beddoe explains another pitfall: 'The intervention by NGOs, is essential but in longer term view, in financial side, funding is the major problem of not to keep continuing the longer term programme. The lack of funding makes it difficult to continue although they need t have a big picture.' For instance, Mr. Flamm tells the story of his neighbour: 'There is a young girl who lives at my apartment building. I think she is around 16 or 17. She has a year-old baby. Her boyfriend is also 16 and still goes to school. She works in a bar full time to support them both while he continues with school. This is their way of life and I doubt it will change. I also know the baby is probably brain damaged as well. When she first learnt she was pregnant, she took some medicine to abort the foetus but it did not work. The child seems to have suffered some impairable brain damage from this. There are many similar cases.'

No single approach, in a single country can solve the problem. There are growing concerns in many countries. In Thailand, in terms of the government's tourism policies, it is likely that the aim was the investment in infrastructure parallel with the sex industry. Then Deputy Prime Minister Boonchu Rojanasathian, advised provincial governors to encourage sex tourism in 1980 saying that: 'We must do this because we have to consider the jobs that will be created for the people. Certain entertainment activities which some of you may find disgusting and embarrassing because they are related to sexual pleasures. Such forms of entertainment should not be prohibited only because you are morally fastidious.'

In September 1992, then Prime Minister Chuan Leekpai sought to crack down on child prostitution and trafficking problem. Two main goals announced at that time were intended as an alternative prevention for the children at risk. As most sex workers come from poor income families where educational opportunities are greatly lacking, this programme sought to improve the standards of educational opportunities, but it did not tackle the problem for the children who are already caught in the web of exploitation. These beginning steps were: to improve the formal and informal education opportunities; to provide vocational training under the Public Welfare Department; and to set up scholarships in poor rural areas under the Ministry of Education.

In Thailand, new amendments to the Penal Code were introduced in late 1996 which include stiffer penalties for the pimps and procurers of children for sexual purposes. The Prostitution Prevention and Suppression Act 1996 seeks harsher punishment imposed on clients', procurers and parents bringing under 18-year-old into the flesh trade. The law punishes everyone involved in the trade, including poor parents who sell their children, middlemen, clients and ring leaders. According to the new law, a jail term of of 2-20 years and/or a fine of 40,000-400,000 baht would be imposed on those having sex with prostitutes under 15-year-old. Procurers and operators who bring children under 18s into prostitution would face a 5-15 years jail sentence and/or a fine of 200,000-400,000 baht. Parents or patrons who conspire with others to allow under 18-year-old to go into prostitution would face similar penalties. Moreover, the bill requires the setting up of an occupation protection and development committee to map out prevention policies, protective mechanisms and measures to equip former prostitutes with the skills to enter other occupations and improve their lives. However, child prostitution in Thailand is actually on the increase because the new law prosecutes everybody. Mr Flamm believes that new laws have just forced the pimps and procurers to change their tactics to go more underground and be hidden from view.

By targeting parents, children and families, they have lost the incentive to provide evidence to aid workers and police that would incriminate the organised criminal gangs running the trade. Another problem is that Thailand and other countries still treat women and child prostitutes as the offenders although they should be treated as victims. The bill also does not answer an old question: why the 1952 Prostitution Prevention Act was never effective. Sanprasit Khumprapan, coordinator of the CPCR explains: 'There is nowhere in the bill to guarantee that it will help improve the situation. The main problem of the prostitution law is not what has been written but how effective it has been enforced. Penalties are harsher, which, in my view, still has nothing to do with enforcement. But all the while, the bill creates more enemies. It tends to look at everybody in prostitution as government enemies, including prostitutes, their parents, and customers. That is why no one would cooperate with police to prosecute procurers and operators because they would be arrested first.'

In the UK, the Sex Offenders Bill was passed in April 1997. This act not only introduces extra-territorial provision for sexual crimes committed against children under the age of 16 overseas, but also requires convicted domestic sex offenders to register their contact details with the police – known as the register of sex offenders. The act includes a double criminality clause which means that the sexual offence must also be recognised as an offence in the country where it occurs. At present, as the act stands, it does not place a requirement on those convicted of sexual offences overseas to register and it does not extend the registration requirement to those offenders who choose to live or travel abroad. This effectively means that children overseas are not as well protected as children in the UK against British sex offenders. It is an offence under British law for UK citizens and residents to engage in underage sexual activity with a child in another country. The penalties are the same as if the offence was committed within the UK. These offences attract severe penalties including a maximum of life imprisonment for some. It is also punishable under British law, for individuals, groups or organisations to conspire or incite others to engage in sexual activities with children. The penalties for organising so-called 'child sex tours' are also severe and may attract life imprisonment. But gathering children's evidence from Thailand or other foreign countries is a difficult task. 'We need police who are specifically trained in dealing with children and cultural norms. International police co-operation as well as police and NGO co-operation will hopefully be the solution to that,' said Ms Beddoe. 'To date, there is no major investigation yet. We are sure this law will work,' she added. Would it be better if paedophiles can be stopped at the airport before flying away? ECPAT UK is now campaigning for an amendment to the Sex Offenders Register. 'Currently, the UK register keeps track of convicted paedophiles when they are in the UK. We want them to add on the offender's address abroad when they travel for work or holiday. We believe that this information can then be passed through the British embassies to foreign police who have been specifically identified as co-operative and how are willing to investigate,' said Ms Beddoe.

Sexual exploitation of children has no easy answers. To improve the situation, since most victims are female, the idea was raised to hire more female law enforcement officers and to raise awareness amongst male law enforcement officers. ECPAT also acknowledges that many law enforcement officials are actively involved in the business, either as customers or directly linked to the trade for financial gain. 'Curbing the number of children entering the sex industry is a vital part of the solution. Resources need to be put into projects that work with communities vulnerable to the sexual exploitation of their children,' said Herve Berger, Executive Director of ECPAT International.

Can child prostitution be eradicated? 'It is hard to measure whether the situation is getting better or not,' confesses Ms Beddoe. 'After all we didn't know the extent of the problem when ECPAT began, therefore any measurement is a hazardous guess. On the one hand, more protective and preventative measure are in place thus hopefully reducing the vulnerability of children to exploitation, on the other hand, new destinations for sex tourism seem to emerge.' Mr Koompraphant Sanphasit, director of CPCR also echoes the sentiment: 'We are only small fish in a big ocean, but we must fight back the best we can and if we band together we can become stronger and force the bigger fish back.' What will be the future look like? 'We should not be satisfied with anything less than stamping it out completely. But it would be unrealistic to think of it being completely wiped out even by the end of the century,' said Ms Abueva of ECPAT former-executive director.

Sidebar 1:

New UK laws: The British government has recently passed legislation which makes it a crime for Britons to engage in sexual activities with children abroad. It is now an offence for UK citizens and residents to engage in under age sexual activity with a child in another country. The penalties are the same as if the offence had been committed within the UK. The offences severe penalties including a maximum of life imprisonment for some. It is also punishable under British law, for individuals, groups or organisations to conspire or incite others to travel overseas to engage in sexual activities with children. The penalties for organising so-called 'child sex tours' are also severe and may attract life imprisonment.

Sidebar 2:

The weak points of law enforcement against trafficking in women and children in Mekong countries include: unclear coverage of cross border trafficking; inefficiency of some laws which cover only sexual trafficking in relation to women and girls and which fail to cover boys (or men); lack of implementation of laws/regulations; slow judicial process; inadequate training of law enforcers to be gender sensitive and child sensitive; insufficient support systems for victims; lack of multidisciplinary team (including psychologists and social workers) to help victims; inadequate provision for the taking of evidence by video; lack of provision to take early deposition of the victims' evidence; weak penalties.

Sidebar 3:

The story of Paweena: Paweena (not her real name) was 13 when she went to work in Bangkok. She is currently taking a vocational training course with the Population and Community Development Association (PDA) in Mae Sai. When she was asked some questions through an interpreter about her previous work, she got upset. She did not want to talk about her own experience. She just wanted to forget about it. She is afraid that other villagers will blame her for worsening the image of village. She said that she could talk about her friends in general. 'The women of her again in the village (she is 20 now) normally go into prostitution after they finish elementary school (aged 13-14 years old) They mostly go to work in Bangkok. After working there for a while, some go abroad, especially to Japan. Some go back to the village. These women might be a mistress of men in Bangkok who will send her money. Some of her friends have not come back yet. They still are in Japan or somewhere in Thailand.'

The story of Lin Lin: Lin Lin (not her real name) from Burma was 13 when she was recruited by an agent to work in Thailand. Her father took $480 from the agent with the understanding that his daughter would pay the loan back out of her earnings. For the next two years, she worked in various parts of Thailand. The owners told her she would have to keep prostitution herself until she paid off her father's debt. Her clients, who often included police officers, paid the owner $4 each time. If she refused a client's demands, she was slapped and threatened by the owner. When the Thai police raided the brothel where she was working, she was taken to a shelter run by a local non-governmental organisation. She was 15, and tested HIV positive.

The story of Ramjai: 'It could have been me. If I couldn't join the Daughter's Education Programme (DEP), I would have definitely gone to work in Bangkok to support my parents,' said Ramjai Jaijoy who is 22. She came to the DEP when she was 13, followed her elder sister. They are the daughters of a rice farmer. Ramjai's parents did not share the beliefs that their daughters were a commodity unlike many others. 'People said my parents

14

have two daughters but the roof of our house is still made of grass. That family has only one daughter, but they have a beautiful modern house. My parents work hard to face their scorn. During the rainy seasons they get up very early to find bamboo shoots and mushrooms. But in 1989, they couldn't support us any longer.' Fortunately, at that time, the DEP started identifying the young girls at risk in her village. They were both accepted into the programme. She wants to continue her education so that she can help the DEP. Now she is working as a DEP office staff, and sending money to her parents.

Sidebar 4:

If you would like to give more opportunities for girls in the North, you may contact: DEP P.O. Box 10 Mae Sai, Chiang Rai 57130 Thailand. Donations can be sent to the Siam Commercial Bank, Mae Sai district branch, account number is 636-206434-8

PREAMBLE

This dissertation aims to look at the issue of 'the child prostitution and tourism' in Thailand. The child sex business is now highly organised, even using the internet to advertise child prostitution. As an extensive literature[1] indicates that tourism is closely related to developments in the sex industry, increases in serious crime of various kinds, and organised gambling. The modes of recruitment of children and the working conditions are inhumane. Such exploitation of children can be explained as stemming from their vulnerable position in society. As a result of entering the commercial sex industry, a new phenomenon, HIV/AIDS, has emerged as a way of life. It is argued that the Asian financial crisis has made children more vulnerable as cheap labourers. It is a vicious circle, however, the tourism industry, built on the sex business in Thailand, has currently become an important source of national income, and the gap between the poor and the rich has become wider even.

The major research questions to be addressed by this dissertation are threefold: The first chapter explains the methodology as well as the decision process of my project. The second chapter focuses on child prostitution in Thailand and also looks at the social and economic aspects. The Thai society and system will be explained together with an outline of the effects of becoming child prostitutes based and Buddhist ideology. Lastly, the third chapter briefly sums up the issue.

---

[1] Lea (1988:69)

CHAPTER ONE: THE PROCESS

The project was aimed at an audience of *Independent on Sunday*, i.e. a serious people who want to be informed about issues and given the background of a topic rather than sensational or negative tourism information. Their awareness on this issue may help change the laws within the UK. I chose these readers as my target group because I talked to Ray Whitaker, the foreign editor of *Independent on Sunday* who seemed very interested in this story idea before I went to the field research.

Before publishing a story, while researching and writing, many decisions have to be made. According to Hausman (1990:4), 'Journalistic decisions are often based on what the reporter feels – by instinct and training – is right. Such decisions typically fall into the following categories: news value, truth, fairness, logic, distortion, legalities, ethics, and the consequences.' The definition of news is varied. Rosenblum (1993:9) notes that news is something which threatens, benefits, outrages, enlightens, titillates, or amuses and people have to see a connection to their own lives (1993:12).

The first decision I made was to decide on a topic. My interest on South East Asia was sparked while I was a university student in 1980s. At the time hundreds of Filipinas came to marry farmers' sons in the remote areas of Japan. This was a plot between the local government in Japan desperate for farmer inheritors, and on the Philippine side, many women who wanted to make money in Japan and supply remittances home, as an alternative to earning as an 'entertainer' or prostitute. The shocking thing was that media coverage treated Filipinas as less than human. This was clearly based on power and gender bias, so I thought readers should have informed free of prejudice. Unfair reports might worsen the diplomatic relations between nations.

After working in Myanmar (Burma) as a field staff member of the Rohingya repatriation programme under the United Nations High Commissioner for Refugees, and as a medical NGO press officer in the Philippines, as well as extensively writing stories and a book on NGOs in the Third World countries, I realised that one of the biggest current problems was the sexual exploitation of children. They face the greatest risk of both contracting the deadly AIDS and damaging their whole life not just physically but mentally.

According to Rosenblum (1993:9); 'There is no shortage of news reports. Each day, we kill a buffalo to eat the tongue.' It is important to look at the factors of making news. As Hausman (1990:11) puts it:

> The first step in deciding what's news is to assess whether it has any immediate effect on readers, viewers, or listeners – whether, for example, it tugs at their

heartstrings, their pocketbooks, or, in the case of actions of civil unrest or war, their desires for safety and stability.

Because of the recent paedophile threat and newspaper coverage in the UK[2], many readers may identify with my subject directly or indirectly although there is a great geographical distance. Considering many children are suffering from abuse by paedophiles both in the UK and abroad, 'child sex tourism' has an immediate and direct impact to readers, whom pressure the government to strengthen the sex offenders' legislation so the subject is very timely. The story involves great magnitude as well. Potentially, it affects or involves many people with children dying from HIV and being mentally damaged because of foreign paedophile tourists including Britons. Considering this, there is a great news value in the subject.

Child sex tourism itself is not a new issue, so I had to focus on the recent phenomenon, such as the effects of the recent Asian financial crisis and new UK extra-territorial laws. Moreover, it has become a highly organised industry in recent years. But most of all, to let British people know the real issues as many are not aware of the child sex tourism in the Far East, which I realised during the research although it involves a large number of British people.

The preparation of the field research began with searching for newspaper articles and books. Before visiting to Mae Sai, Chiang Rai and Bangkok in April, I collected a substantial amount of cuttings. The data was derived from interviews, field research, newspaper articles from local English media, NGO reports (DEP, PDA, CPCR), books, web-sites and the master's thesis on prostitution by Hnin Hnin Pyne (Massachusetts Institute of Technology, 1992).

Interviewing the right people is paramount. I had to meet at least, some girls who used to work as prostitutes, as well as Thai authorities, United Nations agencies, experts from NGOs and academics. I organised some interview appointments while in England. I ended up interviewing three girls in northern Thailand. Interviewing teenagers suffering from mental distress is not easy. They were extra sensitive to strangers. According to Mikel Flamm, a Bangkok-based journalist who helped me with local research: 'The main thing is to listen to what the children have to say but not force them to tell their story. In many cases, they often change their story, often to gain sympathy or at times say what they think you want to hear. So it is best to ask questions from social workers who may have worked

---

[2] e.g. Bournemouth officials say police report is alarmist, The Times, 25/08/98, An international child pornography club run on the internet in East Sussex, The Independent, 03/09/98

with them especially if they are in drop in centres or shelters for street children or abused children.' Mr Flamm also points out that it is hard for a man to interview abused girls. They are very shy and scared so it is better for a woman to do the interviewing. However, it is not easy for anybody to talk and listen to children with severe psychological problems. As my interview with Paweena shows, it may have been a 'salt in the wound'. Mr Flamm spoke of one journalist's experience: 'When a girl was interviewed the first thing he did was to ask the girl how it felt to be raped and being forced to be a prostitute. This was all it took to set her off. She sank into her chair and began to cry uncontrollably. The World Vision social worker who did the interpreting apparently had ask her the question the journalist has asked without thinking over what he had said. The girl began to shake and cry, they ran out of the room. It took a long time before she calmed down.'

On the other hand, Ramjai whom I interviewed, was quite used to talk with strangers as she has already met so many foreigners. It is true that she wasn't actually a prostitute. But she knew exactly what she had to say.

When you talk to local people, another crucial point to consider is that people tend not to talk about something negative about their country because it can make the local situation seem worse abroad. In order to find the right people to talk to, I walked around and looked for bars frequented by Western people and also meeting places in Mae Sai and Chiang Rai. I met an English paedophile in Chiang Rai, talked to him, and got some comments. It proved to be a lucky break. It takes time to build credibility when you ask such sensitive questions. I had to stay in the bar for a while on my own and had to endure the atrocious way as those men/tourist people treated me as if I was a local prostitute looking for a client.

It is likely that people on the different sides tend to say different things. For instance, the Thai government and NGOs. The issue is really complex so they are seeing the same situation from different angles. NGOs obviously are on the victims' side. They know the suffering of children as they are being mentally and physically abused, murdered by traffickers, or dying from AIDS. The government wants to focus on the positive side of the story of course if it is going to be published abroad. They do not want to damage the reputation as a great tourism destination. In this respect, they have different blueprints and it is almost impossible to discuss the same issue. All I could do was to get comments as broadly as possible.

In order to interview the right people, having the right contacts is most important. I have an experience of working in the area, and had some local friends. Without their help, I could not have done all the things such as organising trips and making phone calls to the right people, where local people generally do not speak English and public transportation is not reliable. I went to the go-go bars in Nana Plaza, Bangkok under escort of Mr Flamm. It was almost impossible to enter those places without his company. I could see how those men were enjoying themselves in the almost free bars and how hard those girls were working. This was not the first time to see them but after interviewing girls in the north and researching the background thoroughly, I observed the whole picture differently. For instance, their patience stems from religious belief.

As for privacy issue, Hausman notes: 'there is no justification for publicising embarrassing details of a private person's life just for the sake of publishing a lurid story.' (Hausman, 1990:116) But the public need to know the topic I chose, because something has to be done in foreign countries. They may change the plight of children's situation. When this story is represented by the media, there are two factors which may influence: NGOs' fund-raising and awareness of British people of the need to change the laws in the UK. In this sense, journalists can be defined as parasites. Benthall (1993:9) pointed out in his book, *Disasters, Relief and the Media*, that journalists are sometimes parasitic on human suffering. But the same is true of humanitarian workers, of doctors and indeed of anyone who writes a book. He also reveals (1993:9):

> Everyone should keep in mind two principles: first, that it is for the sake of victims and survivors of disasters themselves that sophisticated systems of communication and assistance should be designed; and second, that in the efforts to relieve suffering, a huge contribution is made by people who never receive public recognition or appear in the media.

For instance, it is likely that world politics is affected by political and economic relations among nations. In this regard, NGOs play an important part in increasing public awareness, focusing the attention of the media and world leaders, on key topics as well exerting pressures on governments. In that sense, in order to change the plight of those children, ordinary people can be a powerful catalyst through media coverage.

Mr Whitaker, foreign editor of *Independent on Sunday*, agrees that journalists have to take the victim's side somehow because their role is not only reporting the facts but to help to combat against evil in the society. You need to get comments from both sides and be fair as much as possible. However, it is not easy to get comments from both sides. From my experience during Rwandan civil war in 1994, it was very easy to get comments without risk from victims, eyewitnesses or NGOs in former Zaire but not from the authorities. When I asked a question to a Zairean officer, his mood got worse and I was held for two hours at a checkpoint in Bukavu, a border town with Rwanda. As for this project, I couldn't meet the owner of brothels who typically had mafia connections. Knowing the situation, I told the local people that I really wanted to meet a brothel owner, but everybody refused because it was too dangerous. I thought I couldn't leave Mae Sai without seeing anyone and finally I persuaded a male local aid worker who had a motor bike to roam the areas. I was advised by many people not to get off the motor bike or stop in front of the brothel, otherwise pimps would get violent either kick me or throw stones at me. Basically, local aid workers didn't want to get in trouble. I couldn't push them asking further because I had to consider the security of local people and myself. It would have been better to put some comments of a brothel owner, but there was no point in taking a great risk. So I tried to be balanced, accurate and objective through plenty of locals' and eyewitnesses' comments and information. Another thing to consider is that it is necessary to have some extra money in a place where bribery is rife.

I was under pressure of deadline as I stayed only two weeks in the field. There were two main difficulties. Firstly, interviewing former prostitute girl was a difficult task. I was in a moral dilemma talking to a girl who had been through a horrible experience. I talked to myself - what is going to happen if I ask these questions and get comments from her? These kinds of things were already done by lots of journalists, and many people noticed that nothing is going to change unless there is a drastic modification. Am I torturing her? I felt so bad and I also felt guilty that I might be the abuser. I could meet at least one girl so I thought that's enough for the project. Another obstacle was interviewing a procurer or brothel owner. As I already mentioned, it was too risky and needed bribery. An alternative was made by finding the tourism brochure or sex tourism information from web-site and books on how to procure girls. This was the safest way an didn't harm anybody.

Secondly, there were many technological and logistical issues such as local phones were not working; or not understanding answerphone messages in Thai; receiving wrong information or addresses due to the language misunderstanding; taxi driver to took me to the wrong places, amongst other things. When I faced those problems and difficulties, I usually asked my local friends for help. Many problems were solved by them. They were my good interpreters at the same time. I've known this country for ten years but the hot weather with 39-degree temperature made me listless and lethargic. For that reason, things which I couldn't complete in Thailand had to be followed up through e-mail back in England. Basically, I used most interviews for this project as I didn't have much choice to choose from. I asked certain questions for industry specialists so there was no information which wasn't reliable or not very important. I researched a lot before interviewing people so there was not a big gap between expectation and reality. If I will follow up this story, I would like to concentrate on the internet issue. The UK is keen on the prevention. It is said that the internet functions in a more underground and professional way which can make things worse. It is apparent that combating organised child sex business through the internet is one of the most challenging tasks of the century.

CHAPTER TWO: THE CHILD PROSTITUTION

2:1 CHILD SEX TOURISM

In order to analyse child prostitution, it is important to know the definition of a child. The principal legal reference is the United Nations Convention on the Rights of the Child (1989), Article 1 defines a child as: 'Every human being below the age of 18 years unless, under the law applicable to the child, majority is attained earlier.'

According to End Child Prostitution in Asian Tourism (ECPAT), a Bangkok-based Non-governmental organisation (NGO), child prostitution refers to the sexual exploitation of a child for remuneration in cash or kind, usually but not always organised by an intermediary (parents, family members, procurers, teachers, amongst others) put another way, it is the act of engaging or offering the services of a child to perform sexual acts for money or other consideration (i.e. gifts or food).

Commercial sex workers had been existed in Thailand at least since the 15th and in general Thai men have a habit of going to the brothels from their early teens. However, the origin of the large scale systematic sex industry started with the R&R (rest and recreation) by GIs, or American soldiers. The number of commercial sex workers is believed to have greatly increased since the late 1960s and the phenomenon is attributed in part to the creation of demand by the United States military in Thailand during the Vietnam War and later by international sex tourism. It is also attributed in part to economic development policies which promoted industrialisation and the provision of services in Bangkok and the Central region at the expense of the agricultural sector (Wawer, et al, 1996).

As a high-performing Asian economy, Thailand experienced a boom in both foreign investment and manufactured exports. According to the World Bank (1993:142), direct foreign investment more than tripled between 1980 and 1988, accompanied by a burgeoning of a middle class of urban consumers, and an increase in rural-to-urban migration of young adults seeking jobs. There is no doubt that commercial sex workers and various associated activities are a now major sector of the Thai urban economy.

While industrialisation is rapidly flourishing in urban areas, rural poverty is still significantly visible. Canadian International Development Agency (CIDA)[3] found that Bangkok's prosperity contrasts sharply with the poverty of the Northeast, an area of the country where income inequality and regional disparities have not improved and 23 percent

---

[3] http://w3.acdi-cida.gc.ca

of the population lives below the poverty line. The proportion of the poor in the Northeast increased substantially from 35.7 percent to 40.7 percent during 1992 and 1994[4]. Korten (1996) has expressed a similar view that there is little evidence that economic growth alleviates poverty. He claims that since 1950 the world's total economic output has increased five-fold while the number of people living in absolute deprivation has doubled. Therefore, as a result of increasing poverty in rural areas, many young women have migrated to urban areas to earn higher wages. The child sex industry is now highly organised and sophisticated. It is impossible to find exact figures due to the nature of business. But ECPAT estimates for the number of children involved in the sex industry could be as high as 800,000 children worldwide.

Circumstance peculiar to holidays, combined with attitudes to places and people identified as foreign, may easily lead to the sexual exploitation of children by tourists, especially in 'exotic' destinations where Western visitors think that the use of children somehow more acceptable than in their home country. Child sex tourism often involves cultural misunderstandings: child abusers convinced that what they do cannot be prejudicial to their victims, justify themselves by saying that they are economically helping the children and their families. This power relationship suggests child sex tourism as a sexualised form of neo-colonialism and racism based on the assumption that young girls in Asia are 'different' from white European girls and more 'sexual', according to ECPAT.

Table 1: The foreign nationals convicted for sexual offences against children in South East Asia[5].

	Number of abusers arrested 1989-93	1989-96
USA	40	59
Germany	30	39
Australia	25	30
England	22	32
France	12	20
Japan	8	20
Canada	8	10

---

[4] http://www.bkkpost.samart.co.th

[5] They were arrested in Southeast Asia.

23

The child sex industry, which sees the child as a commodity, is bound to have deep psychological effects on the young victims. Children involved in prostitution usually experience feelings of guilt and low self-esteem (ECPAT UK Student pack 1996:21). Some children use a euphemism such as 'receiving guests' instead of 'prostitution' as prostitution as such is stigmatised and unacceptable in Thai society. Violence from clients, as well as pimps or madams, is a regular feature of the lives of child prostitutes. Sexual acts also can easily damage their small or immature bodies and make them more susceptible to sexually transmitted and other diseases. Sexually transmitted diseases are the most common medial consequence of child prostitution – amongst them, HIV is the most serious of them. Children in the sex industry are more susceptible to infection with HIV than adults (WHO, 1995:49).

2:2 FACTORS BEHIND THE RISE OF PROSTITUTION

There are two main aspects of commercial sexual exploitation of children: the first one is the demand from the abusers, be they locals or tourists. And the second is the supply, the social, cultural, economical factors that drives children into the sex industry.

First, poverty is a major catalyst for both on demand and supply sides of the sex industry. The majority of children involved are coming from poor, marginalised families. Globalisation, urbanisation and environmental degradation have meant structural changes of families, and rural communities who have, in turn, became more vulnerable to the effects of poverty and exploitation.

Second, gender bias and traditional perceptions of women and girls as being less valuable than boys or men (Muecke, 1992: 891). The lenient Buddhism philosophy dominates the Thai way of life in terms of helping they poor family. Some 85 percent of the population in Thailand belong to the Theravada Buddhism sect. The influence of Buddhism can be seen in all parts of society. The Buddhist ideology of merit making helps commercial sex workers rationalise their work as helping their poor family financially, and local men are helping poor women and their families, i.e. all people are gaining merit for their deeds. In this respect, being a commercial sex worker is self-sacrificing, submissive working pattern for women in terms of Buddhist moral principles. Truong (1990: 137) finds that the status of a commercial sex worker is not considered a result of sexual impurity, but karmic impurity. According to the Buddhist thought, sex is not a sin which is tied to the natural world, the world of suffering and ignorance (Truong, 1990: 134).

In terms of feeding the family, women and daughters have a responsibility to the household economy. Women can be seen as pragmatic and can bear reverses and injustices without injury to their spirit (Mi Mi Khiang, 1984:17) because the sum of merit depends on how much they suffered in this passive philosophy. Therefore, commercial sex can also be seen as merit making for female children who are helping their family and men who are helping women and their families financially.

A belief that boys are mischievous and men irresponsible exists whereas girls are dutiful in Thai society. Such gender differences are assumed to be natural in local Buddhism. Children are raised with the expectation that men need sex, and good girls control their sexuality. This means there are not only bad and good girls working as prostitutes but there are 'justified and unjustified' prostitutes as well who make a lot of money. Muecke (1992:898) points out that remittances and donations tacitly earn them the privilege of hiding their identity as prostitutes from their families and villages. I witnessed many girls in Nana Plaza who prayed before starting 'work' to an alter in front of go-go bars. This blind support system makes girls justified. The remittances help parents' finance and siblings' school tuition fees, donating to temples, then giving them 'good girl' status with family or relatives.

Though many sympathisers tried to defend the parents for reasons of economic necessity, the fact remains that these parents were principally responsible in dictating the lives and futures of their 10-year-old daughters, even before their menstruation, selling their bodies in order to save the family from financial crises. Many parents naively believe that their daughters are now in good hands, even when the parents come to visit them in well-established brothels and call girls' dormitories run efficiently by well-to-do agents in respectable surroundings. However, not a few of them already know the truth and prefer to believe that they have sacrificed their daughters for a good cause, i.e. to provide the families with the necessities of life. (Muecke, 1992: 898)

This cultural analysis shows that the ideologies of the family and women's support system have not been changed by the growth of the sex trade in Thailand. In reality, selling daughters ensure their good status through direct consumption of consumer goods for parents, siblings, or merit making.

CHAPTER THREE: CONCLUSION

As evidence suggests, the aim of the government's tourism policies was the investment in infrastructure that went in parallel with the sex industry. According to official sources, in 1987 at least 248 hotels in Bangkok, hosted commercial sex workers as a means to increasing gross income (quoted by Truong, 1990: 167). As I quoted in my project, then Deputy Prime Minister Boonchu Rojanasathian, claimed that entertainment should not be prohibited only because one was morally fastidious (Muecke, 1992).

The existed child sex business was exacerbated by foreign tourists. They are taking advantage of children by justifying themselves. Commercial sex workers are connected to various economic activities in the formal sector, such as creating extensive employment opportunities for non-commercial sex workers such as taxi drivers and restaurants who are now a stable source of income. The trafficking in children has emerged as a border trade in a process for seeking shortcuts of investment without capital in the process of development.

To make girls stop working, careful planning is necessary. Because they have no idea what to do. As short-term strategies, finding alternative job opportunities, providing vocational training and educational support for girls with high-risk can be important just like the Daughter's Education Programme activities. There are lots of sceptical opinions on vocational training but it is apparently a positive opportunity for them as they are benefitted from learning discipline. As long-term strategies, men and women in each country need to be educated to realise that using child prostitute is morally wrong and destroys the lives of children. Women's (mother's) empowerment, and changes in the attitudes and sexual behaviour of men through education are urgent solutions. Education programmes alone may not necessarily provide a release from poverty or immediately change the system such as improving living conditions, moreover, it takes time for the effectiveness of education to be seen. However, it will be a great catalyst for social change in the long run.

Finally, what I learned from the research is: it cost a lot of money as you need to pay for interpreters, drivers and bribe in developing countries. If I had enough money for bribery, I probably could have met a brothel owner (it is impossible to meet these kind of people without paying extra money in order to protect yourself and your companions); you need to spend some time to build up a good relationship or earn trust somehow when asking sensitive questions to victims; if you have many friends, especially more than contacts, they will help you a lot to meet the right people. It works especially in Asia because they greatly value personal relationships. For instance, when you end up in a place you have no idea. If you can afford it, it would be a good idea to hire a local assistant. It may be useful if you go to the local bars and make yourself approachable so that you can get extra information unexpectedly.

Especially in the case of my topic, apart from having knowledge on the issue, it is important to know the Thai society and culture as the whole child prostitutes issue is strictly related to their way of life. In that sense, it is essential to learn the connection of two countries including the historical relationship. The way interviewing people in Southeast Asia is also different from Europe. They are not going to open their mind if one asks straightforward questions. Most of the cases, especially the girls who have been having a tough time, the Western sense of dialogue does not apply. In this regard, choosing the right interpreter is paramount.

I think I did and wrote almost everything I wanted to write. I am happy with the result. I hope readers will react to the story and take action.

INTERVIEWS

Face to Face

Chris Beddoe: campaign co-ordinator of ECPAT UK, 02/03/98, London

Chitraporn Vanaspong: information officer of ECPAT International, 12/04/98, Bangkok

Atchara Chan-O-Kul: press officer of the Centre for the Protection of Children's Rights in Bangkok, 16/04/98. Bangkok

Mikel Flamm, freelance journalist, 12/04/98, Bangkok

Sompop Jantraka, director of Daughter's Education Programme, 01/04/98, Mae Sai

Sanprasit Khumprapan, co-ordinator of CPCR, 16/04/98, Bangkok

Mark King, British businessman, 17/04/98, Kuala Lumpur

Prakran Nilnet, local aid worker, 03/04/98 Mae Sai

Jeremy Ruggrok, British paedophile, 05/04/98, Chiang Rai

Barinthip Sirorat, chief of foreign relations subdivision, Department of Public Welfare in Thailand, 16/04/98, Bangkok

Wanlop Pichipongsa, operation officer of Population and Community Development Association, 06/04/98, Chiang Rai

Paweena, girl at PDA, 06/04/98, Chiang Rai

Ramjai Jaijoy, DEP staff, 02/04/98 Mae Sai

Phone

Debbie Gibson, press officer of Association of British Travel Agents, 15/07/98, London

E-mail

Seree Wangpaichitr, Tourism Authority of Thailand Governor, 23/07/98

Pasuk Pongpaichit, lecturer of the Faculty of Economics, Chulalongkorn University in Bangkok, 03/08/98

Quotes by permission

Ron O'Grady, chair of ECPAT International

Amihan Abueva, former-executive director of ECPAT International

Koompraphant Sanchasit, director of CPCR

REFERENCES

Asia Watch, et al. (1993) *A Modern Form of Slavery: Trafficking of Burmese Women and Girls Into Brothels in Thailand*, New York: Human Rights Watch

Benthall, J., (1993), *Disasters, Relief and the Media*, London: I.B. Tauris & Co., Ltd

Centre for the Protection of Children's Rights (1996), *Case Study Report on Commercial Sexual Exploitation of Children in Thailand*, Bangkok: CPCR

Centre for the Protection of Children's Rights (1995), *Preliminary Survey on Regional Child Trafficking for Prostitution in Thailand*, Bangkok: CPCR

Department of Public Welfare (1996), *Annual Report*, Bangkok: Department of Public Welfare

ECPAT (1997), *Commercial Sexual Exploitation of Children 1996-1997, A Report on the Implementation of the Agenda for Action Adopted at the First World Congress Against Commercial Sexual Exploitation of Children*, Bangkok: ECPAT International

ECPAT (1998), Newsletter, no22, January

ECPAT UK (1998), Student Pack, London: ECPAT UK

International Herald Tribune, *Young Girls in Supply*, 23/01/1996

Hausman, C, (1990) *The Decision-making Process in Journalism*, Chicago: Nelson-Hall Publishers

Lea, J, (1988) *Tourism and Development in the Third World*, London: Routledge

Korten, D (1996) *Burma: Balance and Harmony in Women in the New Asia: The Changing Social Roles of Men and Women in South and South-East Asia*, Paris: UNESCO

Moser, C (1993) *Gender Planning and Development: Theory, Practice and Training*, London: Routledge

Muecke, M (1992) *Mother Sold Food, Daughter Sells Her Body; The Cultural Continuity of Prostitution*, Soc, Sci, Med, 35.7,891-901

O'Grady, R (1992); *The Child and The Tourist*, Bangkok, ECPAT